My Scrap

ISBN-13: 978-1534688551

ISBN-10: 1534688552

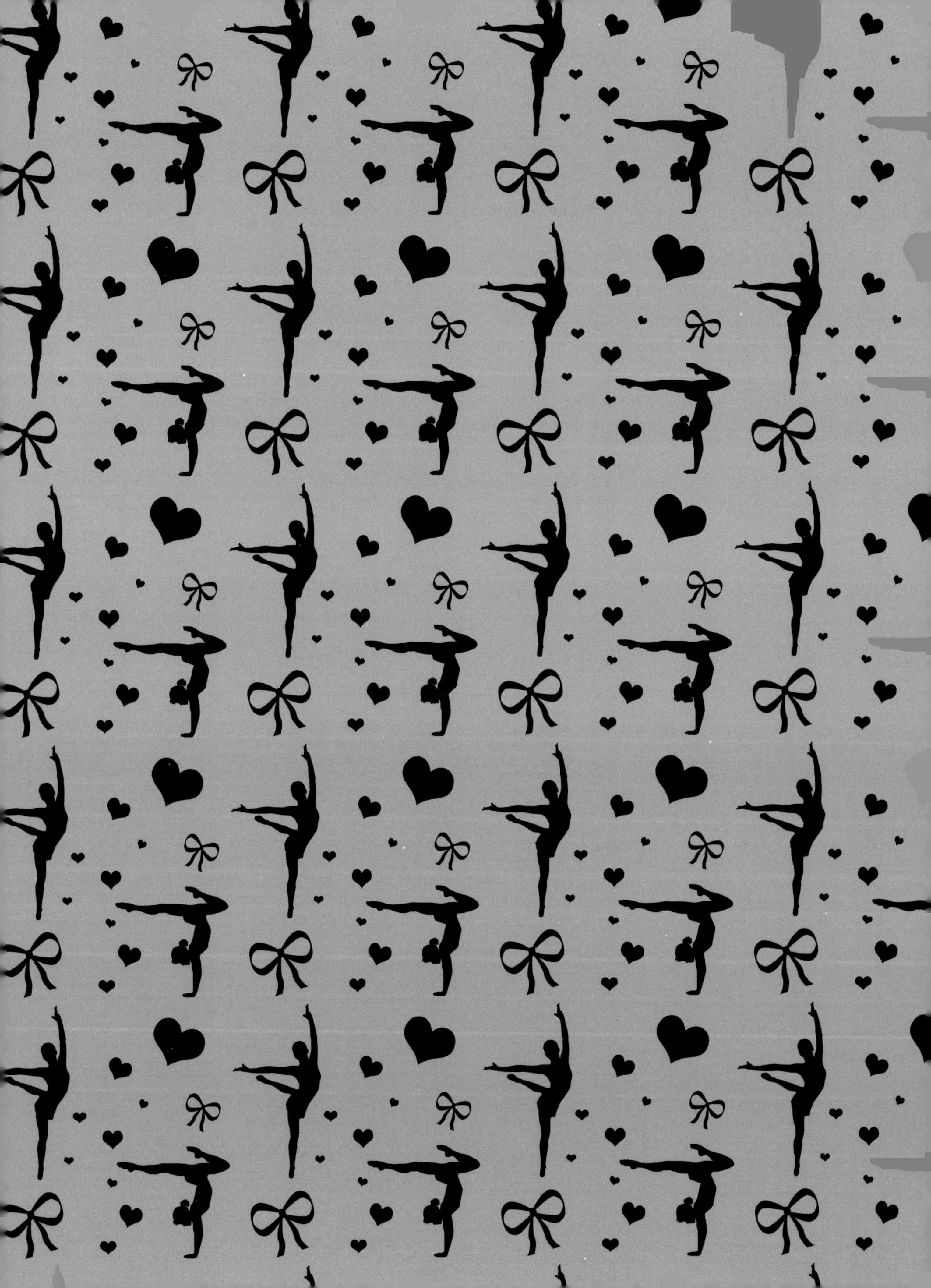

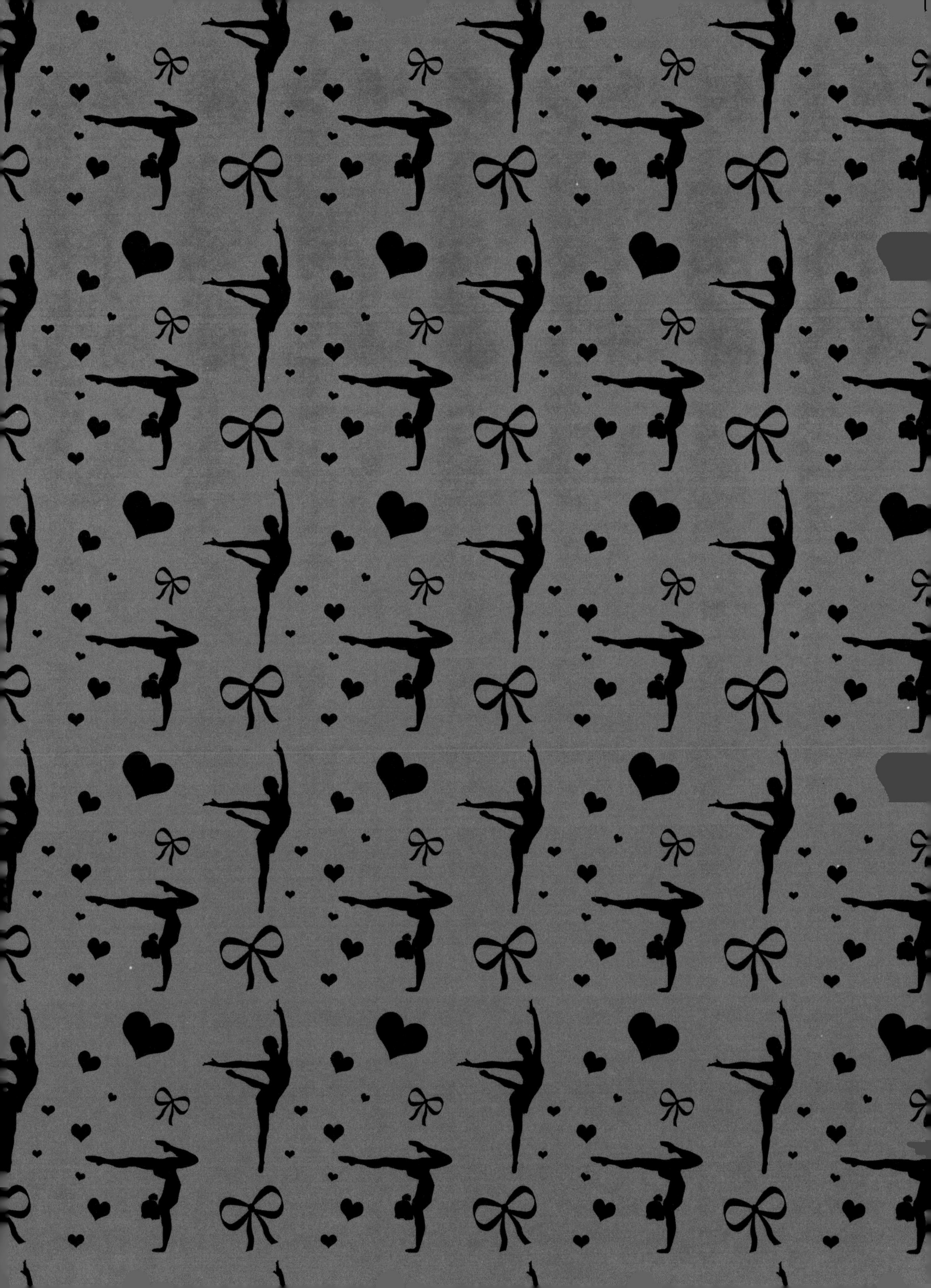

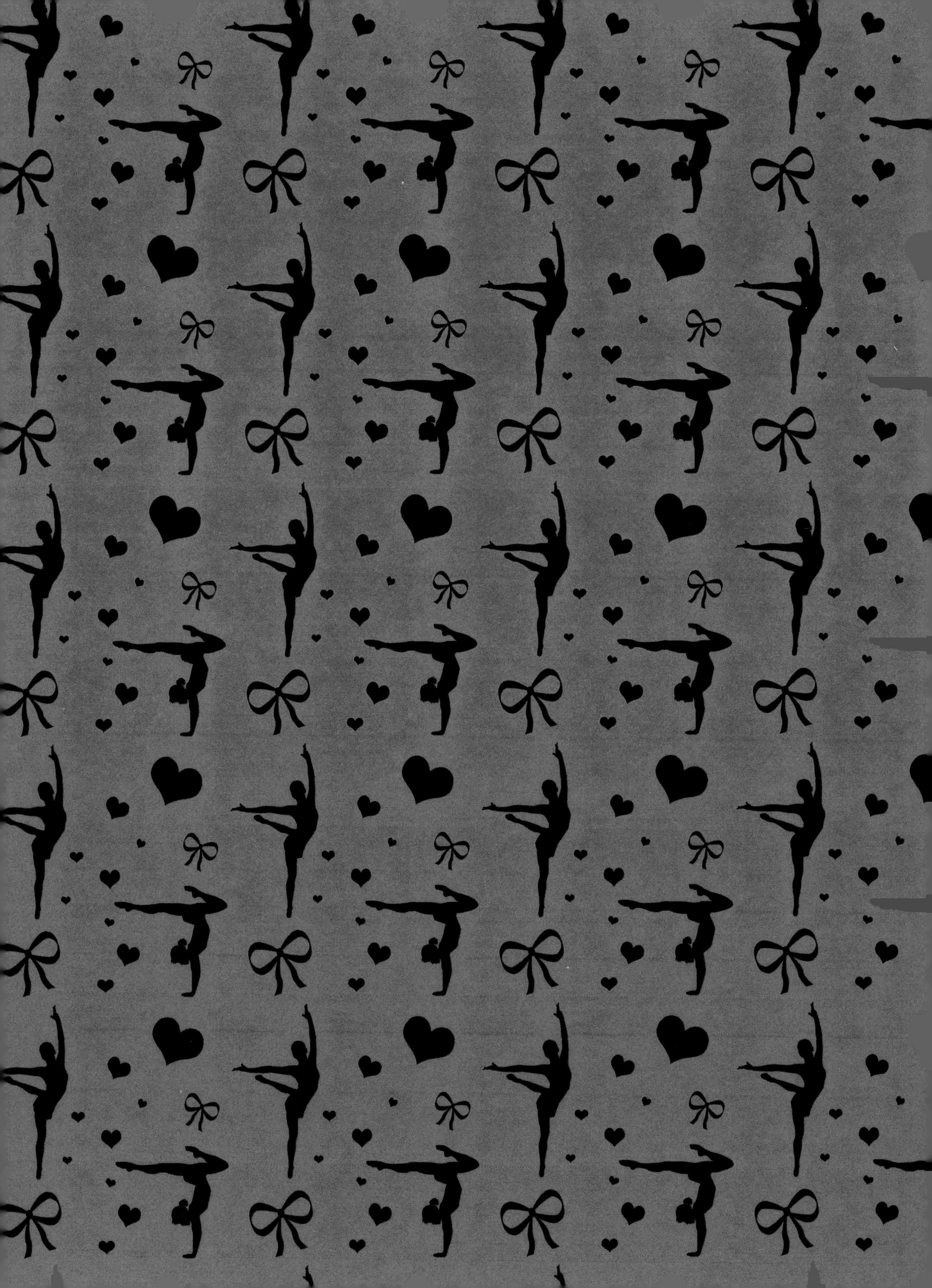

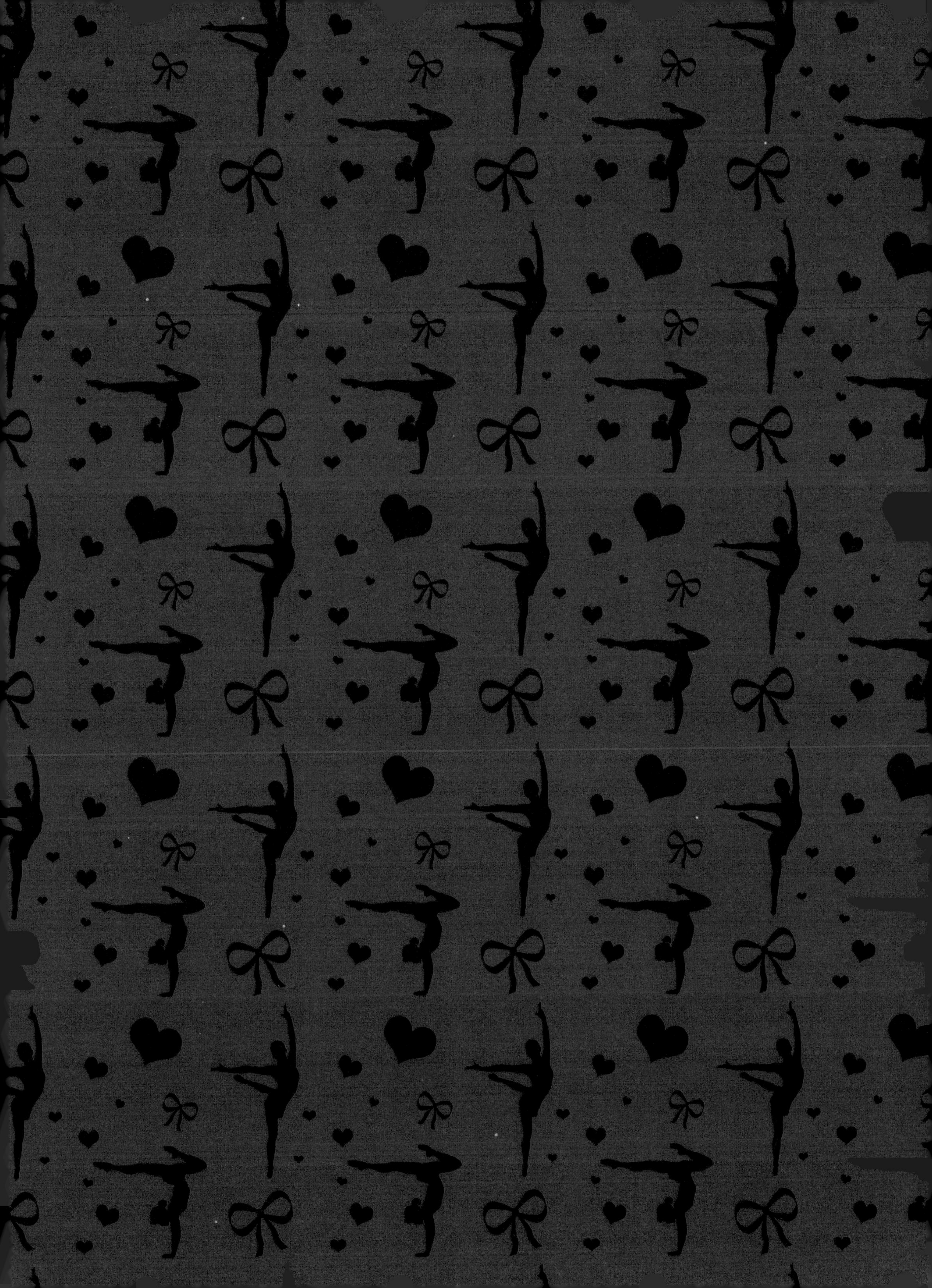

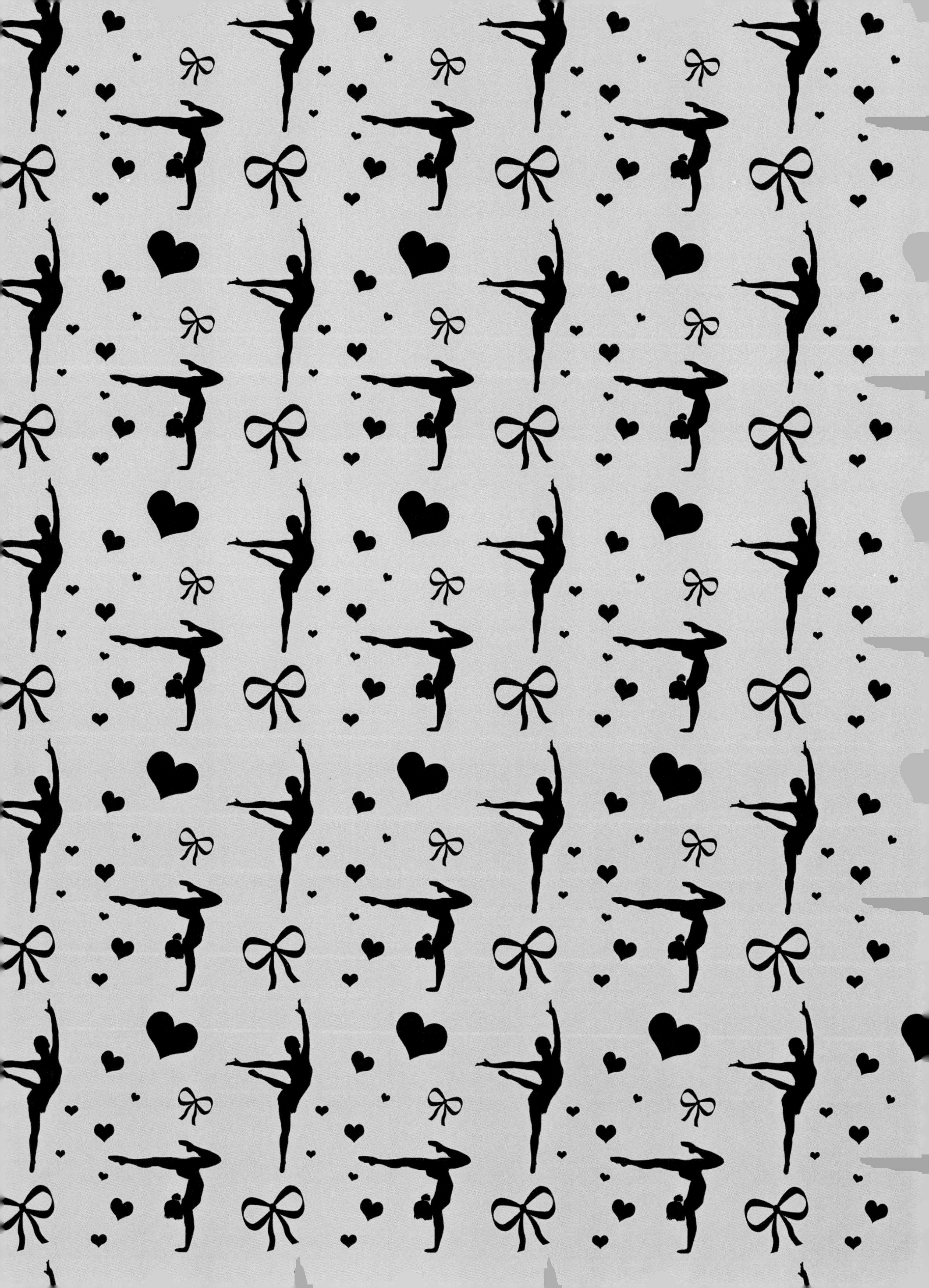

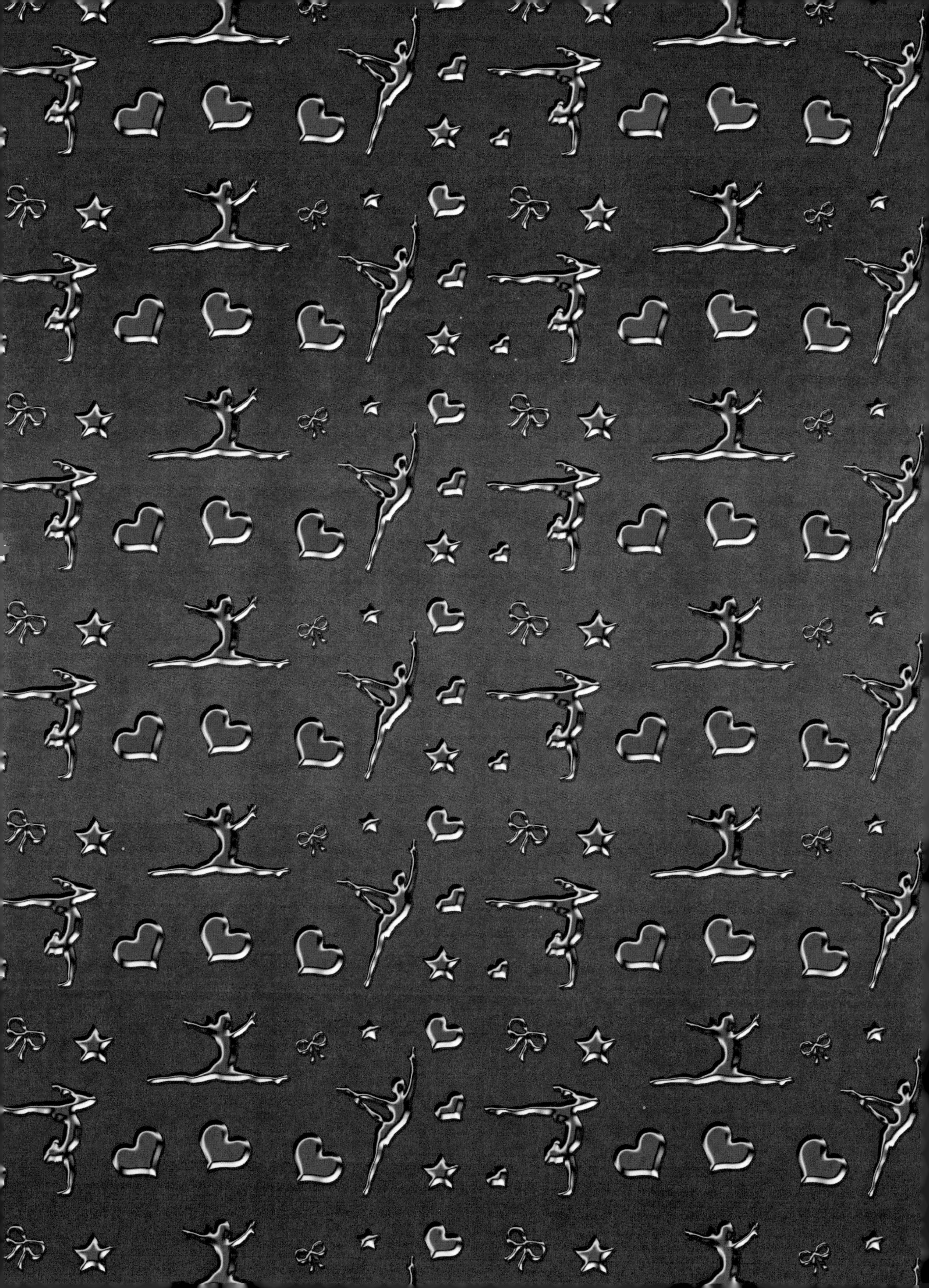

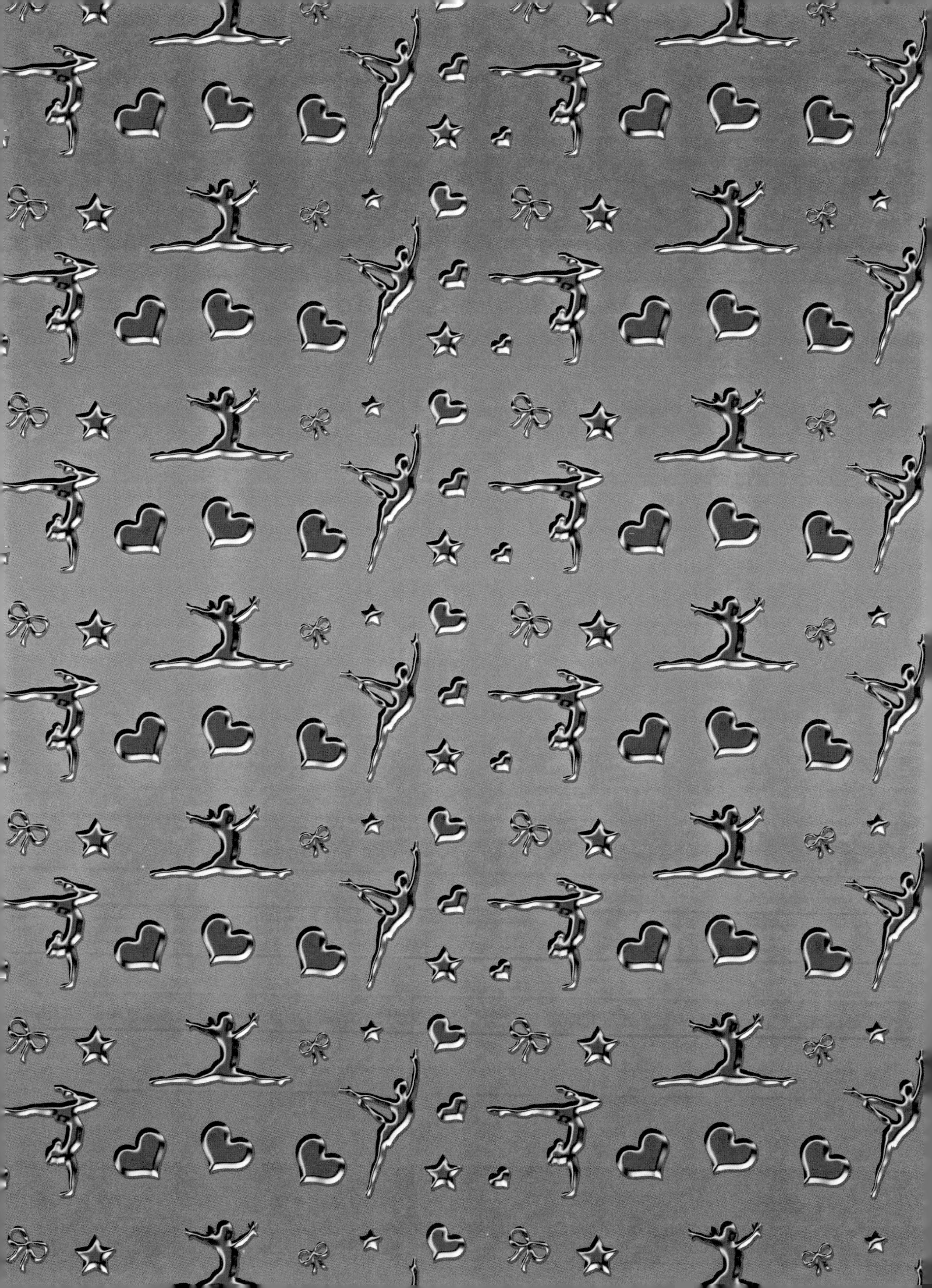

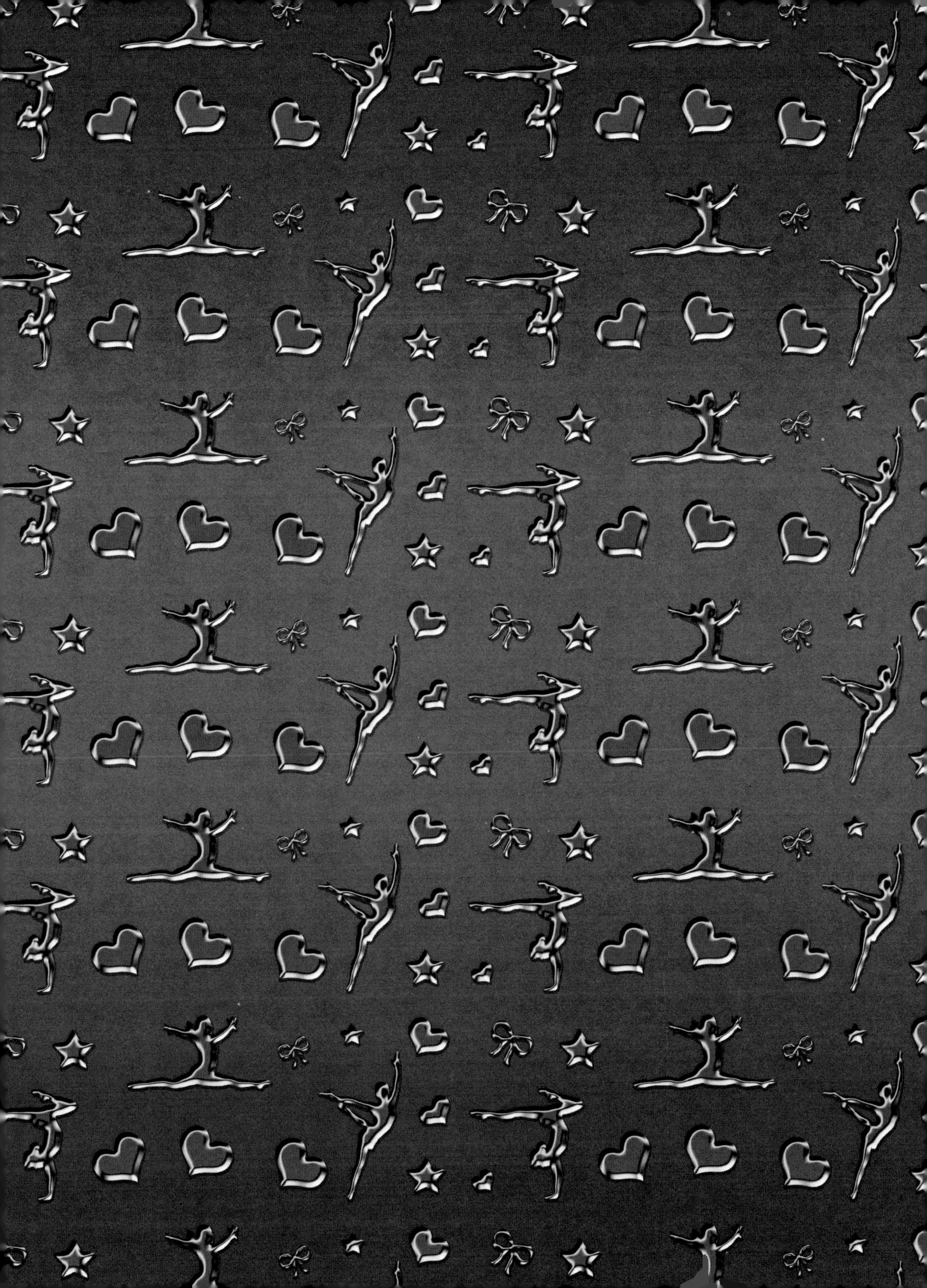

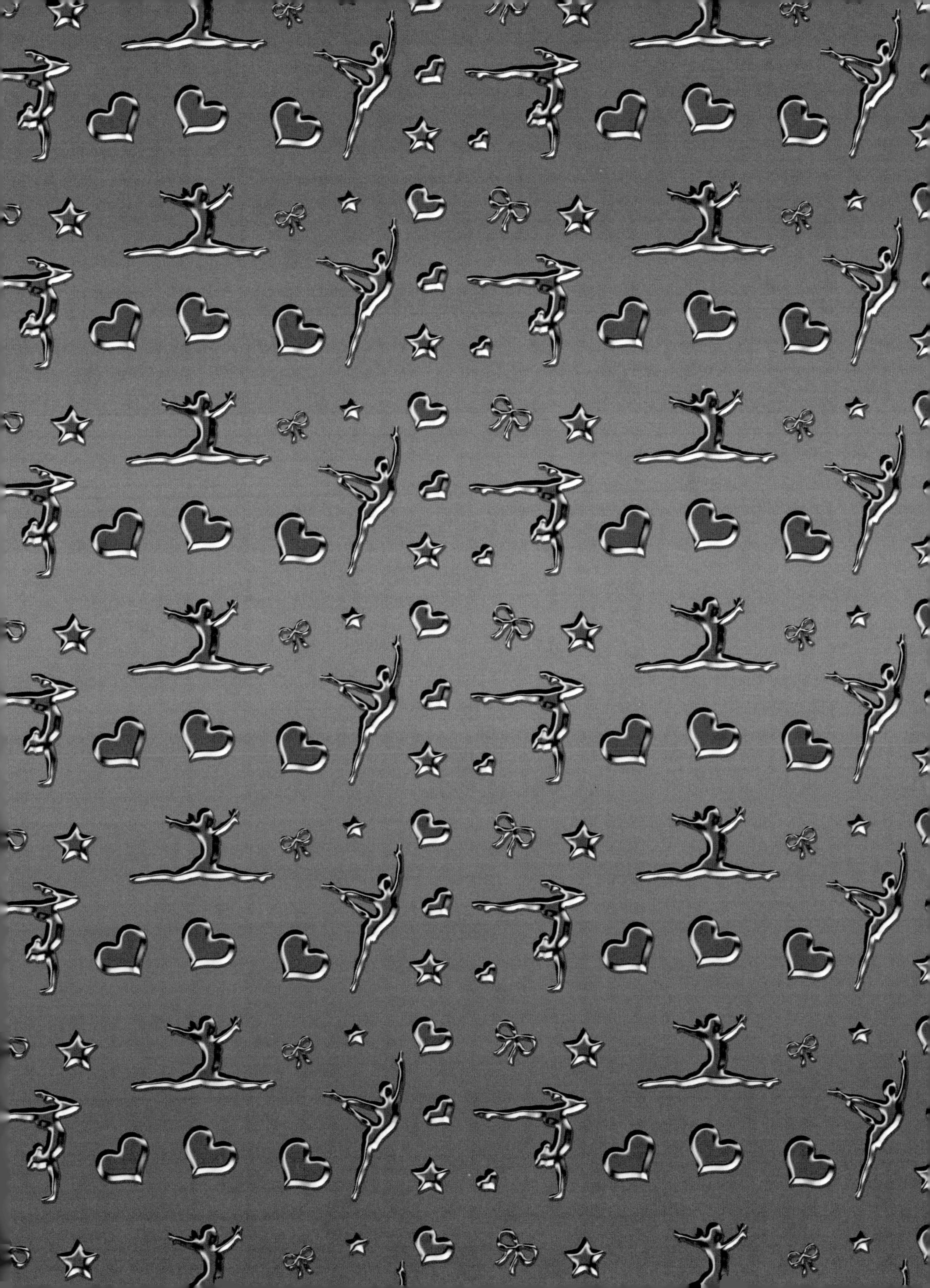

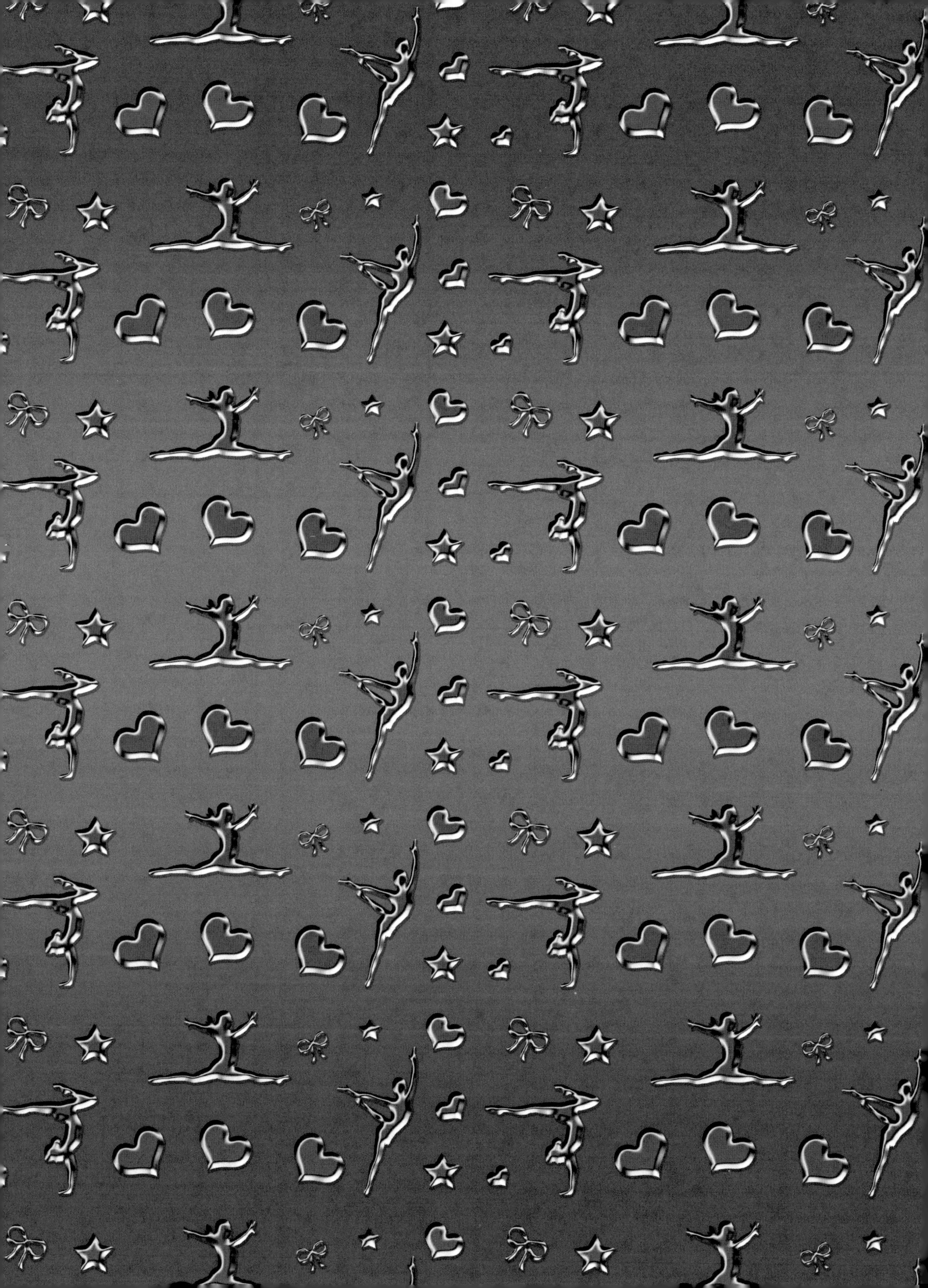

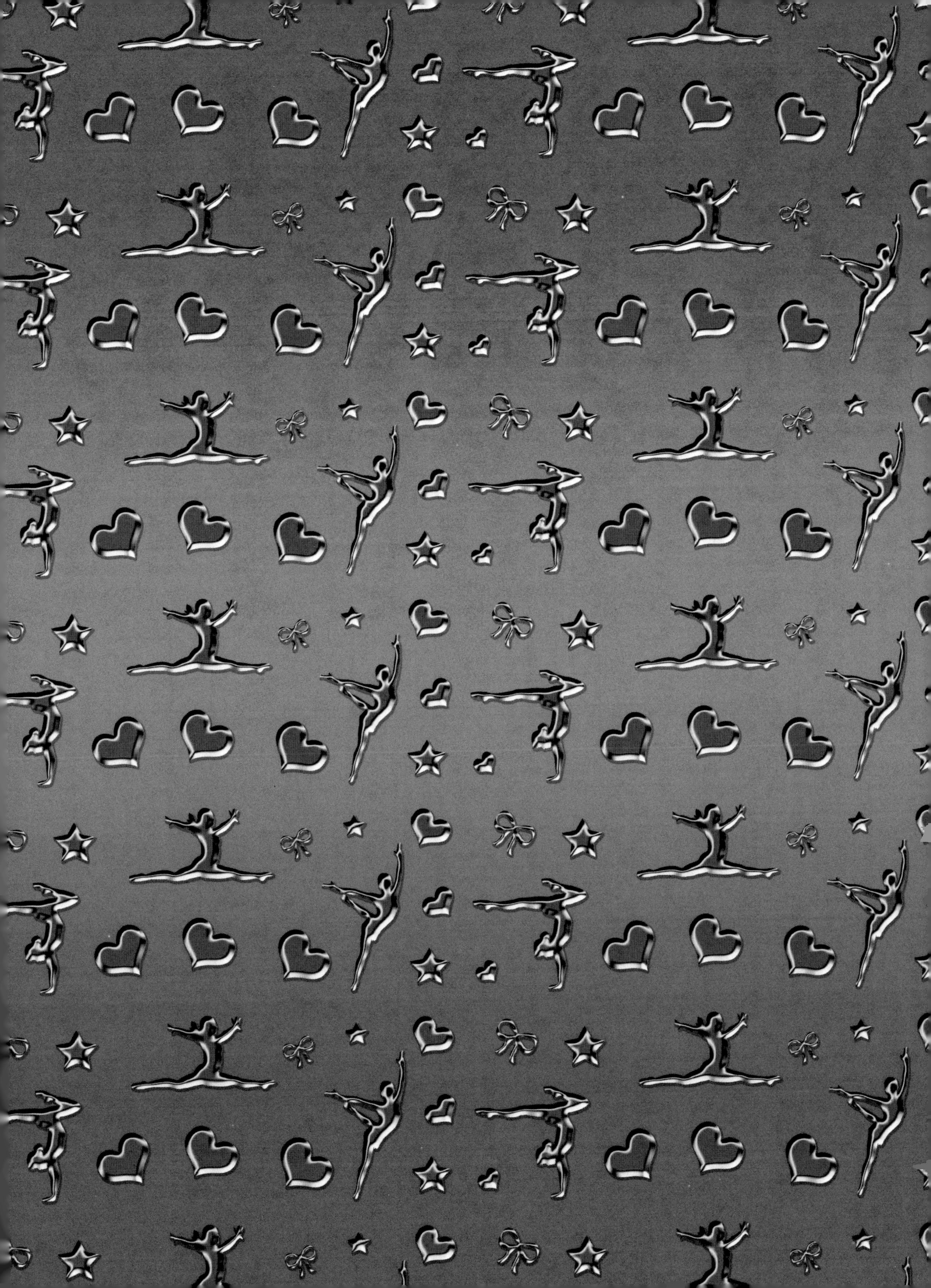

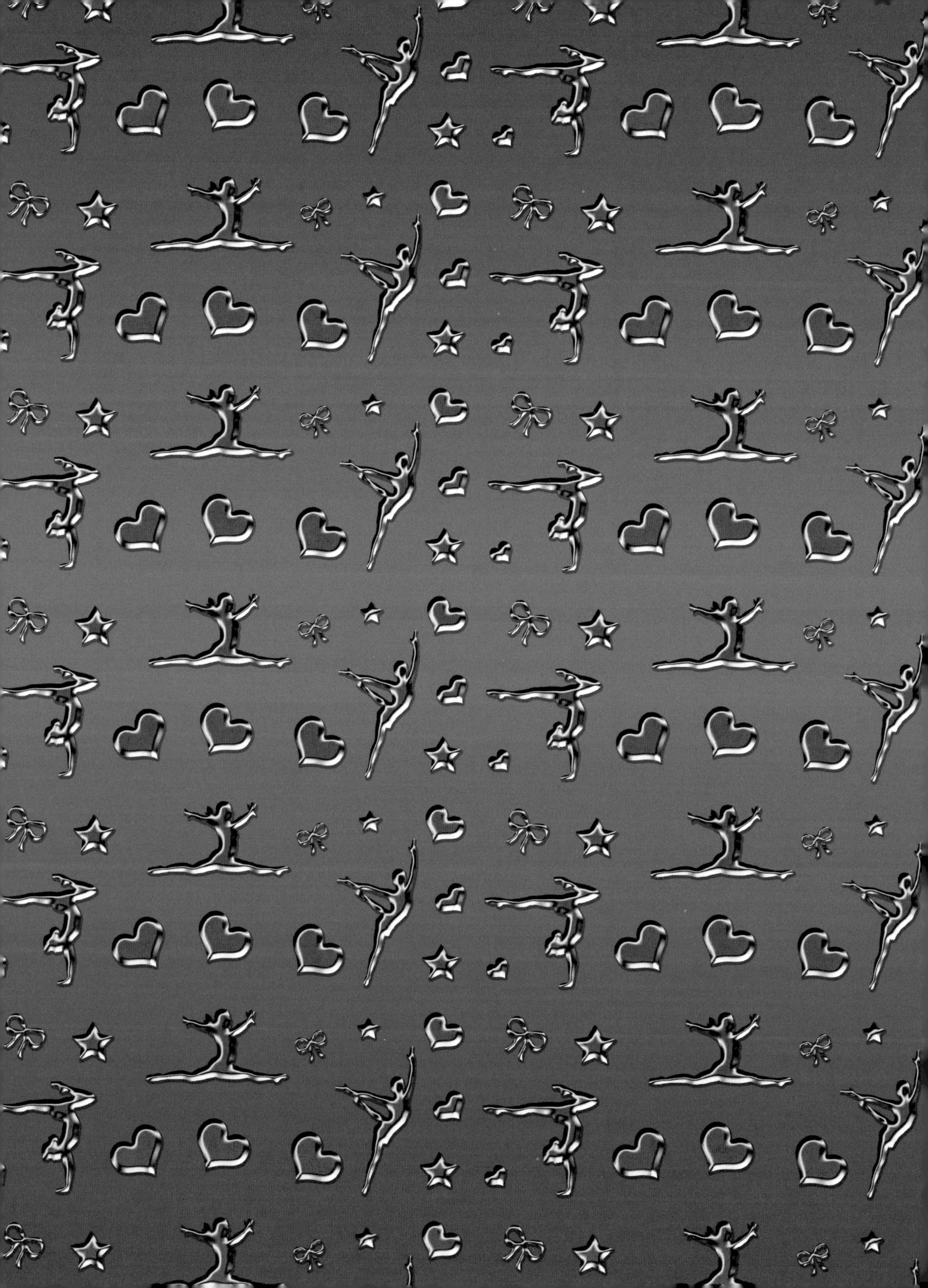

Made in the USA
Monee, IL
30 June 2020

35502003R00026